Habitats

William B. Rice

Consultants

Sally Creel, Ed.D.
Curriculum Consultant

Leann Iacuone, M.A.T., NBCT, ATC
Riverside Unified School District

Image Credits: p.2 Jeff March/Alamy; p.24–25 (background) Christoph Bosch/age fotostock; p.25 (top) F Hecker/age fotostock; p.4 (top) Spirit/age fotostock; pp.9 (top), 11 (top), 18–19, 21, 31 iStock; pp.28–29 Janelle Bell-Martin (illustrations); all other images from Shutterstock.

Teacher Created Materials
5301 Oceanus Drive
Huntington Beach, CA 92649-1030
http://www.tcmpub.com

ISBN 978-1-4807-4601-5

Printed by: 590835
Printed in: China

Table of Contents

At the Bus Stop

You are waiting at the bus stop and see a hippo walking down the street. You are surprised! It's not that the hippo is too big for the bus. The hippo just doesn't belong on your street! Your street is not the hippo's **habitat**.

Where Does It Belong?

The hippo's real habitat is a grassland with calm water.

A hippo's skin gives off a red oil that acts like sunscreen.

What is a habitat? It is the home for a living thing. You might think of a habitat as a living thing's address.

Every living thing has a place that is best for it. The place has what the living thing needs. It can live well there.

Sea stars have many habitats. They do very well along sandy shores.

What Makes a Habitat?

The right habitat for a living thing has just what it needs to live well. This means the right soil, water, food, and light. It means the right **climate**, too. And it means the right **predators**!

Predators

Predators are animals that live by killing and eating **prey**.

A tree frog lives in a rainforest habitat.

Lizards live in the desert, where they enjoy the sun's heat.

Things that live on land need the right kind of soil. Plants need soil to grow. Animals need plants for food. Or they eat animals that eat the plants! Animals also need the right kind of land for their **shelter**.

Plants and animals need water, too. They may need freshwater. They may need saltwater. Plants and animals must live in habitats that have the right kind of water and plenty of it.

This bird drinks freshwater from a river.

Badgers dig burrows in the land.

A barrel cactus grows best in sandy soil.

In the fall, chipmunks store food in their burrows to eat through the winter.

Living things also need the right kind of food. Plants need **nutrients** from the soil. Plants also need **energy** from the sun. Light helps them grow. Some animals eat plants. Others eat meat. Some eat both. They all need plenty of food through the year to live.

Living things need light and energy from the sun.

The Right Predators?

If there are too many of one kind of animal in a habitat, there will not be enough resources to go around. Predators keep animal groups from growing too large.

Every living thing has a climate that is best for its **health**. Some things do well in warm and dry climates. Some things do well in warm and wet climates. Some things do best in cold climates.

Scorpions like living in a dry desert climate.

Living things **evolve** to live in certain climates. Some animals grow thick fur for the cold. Some plants grow deep roots to reach water. Living things have many amazing ways to survive!

Plants on the floor of the rainforest often have large leaves to get as much sunlight as possible.

Where Do They Live?

Each living thing has a habitat that is just right for it. Can you tell why each habitat is right?

Lobsters

Lobsters are found in all oceans. They live on the ocean floor, mostly near the shore. They live in cracks and burrows in rocky, sandy, or muddy areas. They eat sea plants and animals.

Lobsters have hard shells to protect them. As they grow, they shed their shells and grow new ones.

Not Your Usual Habitat!

A **parasite** is a living thing whose habitat is on a host body. The host is another living thing. The parasite survives by living off a host like this parasite attached to a fish.

Brain corals are found in most of the world's oceans.

Brain Corals

Brain corals are small ocean animals. They live in coral groups on the ocean floor. They like warm, shallow water. They stay in one place. Their food floats in the water. Other animals stir up the water. Then, the ocean water moves. This brings the food to them.

Tentacles

During the day, brain corals wrap themselves in their tentacles to stay safe. At night, they reach out their tentacles to catch food.

Bristlecone Pines

Bristlecone pines are tough trees. They grow high in the mountains of dry areas. They grow slowly because it is cold and windy there. Their wood is thick with a lot of sap. This keeps them safe from pests. Their soil has many nutrients in it.

Bristlecone pines can live more than 5,000 years.

Black Widow Spiders

Black widow spiders are found all over Earth. They live under and behind large objects. They like places that are dark, cool, and moist. They weave webs with their sticky silk. They eat insects that get trapped in the webs.

Black widow spiders are mainly black, with a red hourglass spot on their bellies.

Watch Out!

If you see a black widow spider, stay away and tell an adult. Their bites are dangerous!

Raccoons

Raccoons mainly live in forests. However, they are smart and not picky. They have learned to live many places. They even live in cities! They live in small family groups. They eat plants and animals. They use their front paws almost like people use their hands.

Raccoons are good at finding food anywhere.

A raccoon's paws can do many things.

At Home

Every living thing has a home that is right for it. The home has what the plants and animals need to be healthy and well.

We each belong in our own habitat. If you ever see a hippo getting on a bus, tell it to head back to its habitat!

Polar bears have thick fur, which is perfect for a cold, icy habitat.

This mongoose lives in a rocky habitat, where it can eat small snakes and birds.

Let's Do Science!

Can you create a habitat? See for yourself!

What to Get

- ❍ activated charcoal
- ❍ ferns
- ❍ gravel
- ❍ large glass jar with lid
- ❍ moss
- ❍ potting soil
- ❍ water

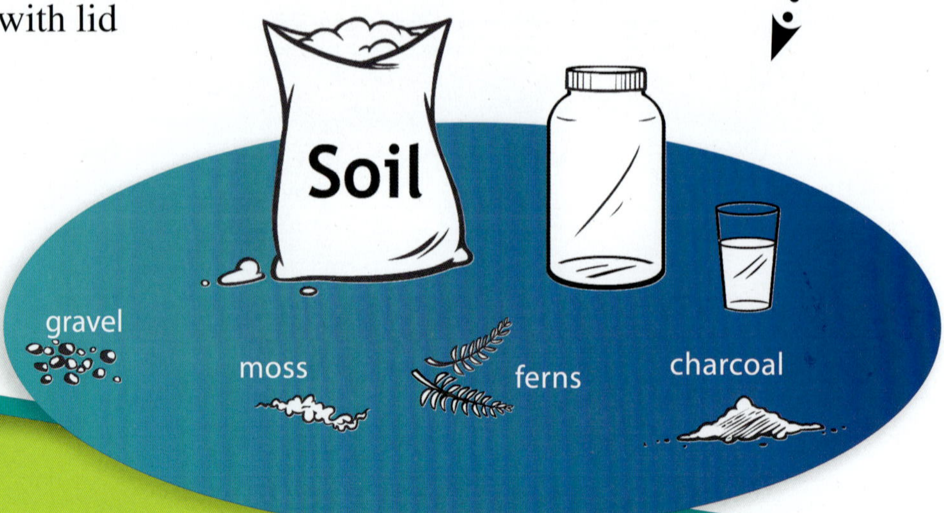

What to Do

1. Cover the bottom of the jar with about one inch of gravel. Add a thin layer of charcoal. Add a layer of soil about two to three inches deep.

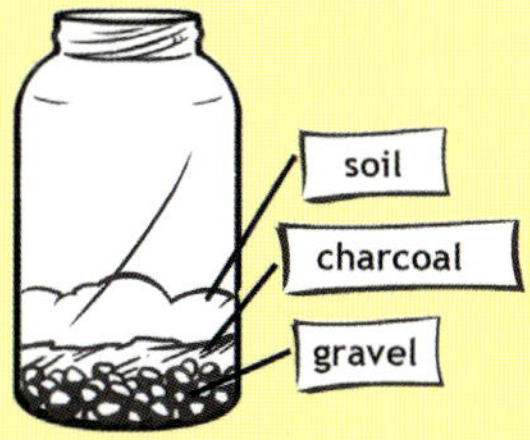

2. Plant small ferns and moss. Plant the largest plants first.

3. Water the plants just a little. Put on the lid to keep the water in. (You will need to add only a few drops of water every few months.)

4. Place the jar in natural light, but not direct light. Observe your habitat. What do you think will happen if you change something in it? Tell a friend.

Glossary

climate—the usual type of weather a place gets

energy—power that can be used to do something

evolve—to change slowly over time to become stronger and better suited to certain conditions

habitat—the place where something lives

health—well-being

nutrients—substances that plants, animals, and people need to live and grow

parasite—a living thing that lives in or on another living thing and gets food or protection

predators—animals that live by killing and eating other animals

prey—living things that are hunted by other living things for food

shelter—a place that covers or protects people or things

Index

Your Turn!

Different Habitats

There are many different habitats right in your own neighborhood. Look for two different habitats. How are they alike? How are they different? Draw a picture of each habitat, side by side.